FIFTEEN WALKS FROM CONISTON AND WINDERMERE

PAUL BUTTLE

Published by

amadorn

I would like to thank the following people for the help they gave me in producing this guide: Lorraine Hodgkinson, Denstone Kemp, Terry Lowe, Pat Clark, Pádraig Ciobháin, and most especially Jonathan Miller for making me mobile and Bill Formby for his suggestions.

ISBN 0 9513717 6 2
© P. Buttle 1993.
Published by Amadorn, 18 Brewery Lane, Keswick, Cumbria.
Typeset by The Keswick Studio, Keswick.
Imageset by McKane Printers, Keswick.
Printed by The Nuffield Press, Oxford.

CONTENTS

INTRODUCTION

This guide covers the southern sector of the Lake District National Park. Until I came to write this guide it was a part of the Lake District that was almost wholly unknown to me, apart from the Coniston Fells. I had ignored it as being far too low lying to bother with. Writing this guide therefore has been something of an exercise in discovery on my own part, and I have discovered some very pleasing delights and a lot of surprises.

I cannot claim then that this guide is a distillation of my own long acquired knowledge of the area. It is not, but in choosing the walks I have I did seek the advice of Bill Formby who lives in the area and knows it far better than I do. Some of the walks took two or three visits to finalise, other walks I eventually decided were not good enough to include. This being so I hope the purchasers of this guide will feel they are gaining something they could not otherwise have obtained through pure serendipity, though serendipity should never be disparaged of course.

This is a more gentle Lakeland to the one I am more familiar with, whose attractions are subtle rather than grand and impressive. I would still advise anyone to explore other parts of the Lake District before exploring this part of it, but unless one explores this part of the Lake District one can never really claim to know it completely. To my mind many of the walks in this guide would make pleasant long summer evening saunters, especially as most of them end at a pub, or they would make good family walks as they are none too long and only three of them involve any real climbing. They should even interest the more ardent walker looking for an easy option on a murky day, or the walker whose more strenuous days on the hill are now over. They are all interesting and nearly all of them reveal an aspect of the Lake District most visitors to the Lake District will be unaware of.

Order of the walks.

As has been my practice in my other guides I have ordered the walks, as much as I could judge it, by the amount of effort each walk requires. So the easiest walk comes first and the hardest last. Apart from the last three walks they are really all country rambles and none too difficult. The final walk, the Coniston Fells, is really out of scale with all the other walks. Because of this I hesitated to include it, but in the end I decided a guidebook with the title I intended this guide to have could not in all honesty exclude such a walk.

Time of the Walks

The suggested time of each walk is just that, 'suggested'. I've tended to suggest what I think is a generous time allowance on the basis that you don't stop. As it is more than probable that most people using this guide will want to stop the suggested times should be adapted accordingly.

Choice of maps.

It is essential to have a map when walking the fells. Only the last three walks in this guide come into that category, but even on the low level walks it would still be better to have a map than to rely solely on the sketch maps provided in this guide. The Ordnance Survey large scale, 1:25,000, Outdoor Leisure Maps 6 and 7 cover only eight of the walks in this guide completely and another three partially, though Map 6 alone does cover the critical three 'fell walks'. Using the Landranger series, 1:50,000, you will need to have three maps, 96, 97 and 89 or 90, to cover all the walks. The best buy therefore is the 'One Inch' Tourist Map of the Lake District, though this has a slightly larger scale than the Landranger series, 1:63,360, (......ah, the beauty of the seeming illogicality of those past imperial measurements!) it covers all the walks in this guide except the Hampsfield Fell Walk, which hopefully you might be able to get away with just using the guide's sketch map.

Safety on the Fells

The last three walks, and especially the last one, are fell walks. Make sure therefore if you go on these walks that you are properly equipped and prepared for bad weather.

Public Transport

At the time of writing I would hazard at least ten of the starting points in this guide are reachable by public transport, and another three come quite close, but the connection times are often of little practicability. Times and routes are also constantly changing and it is therefore difficult to give up to date information. However Cumbria County Council do provide an excellent travel timetable information service called Travel Link, telephone (0228) 812 812, which should be able to answer any queries as to what places are reachable using public transport and how frequent are the services.

Tosnáionn turas fada le h-aon
choiséim amháin

THE RUSLAND VALLEY

Distance	5 miles
Total feet of Ascent	400 feet
Suggested time	2 hours
Starting point	Oxen Park, 7 miles south of Coniston (SD 318 873)
Car Parking	Outside village hall, on the road to Lowick

A countryside ramble over a quiet secluded landscape with a surprisingly varied terrain of heath land, woodland, marshland as well as farmland with prospects of wooded hills all around. There is a public house in the middle of Oxen Park village.

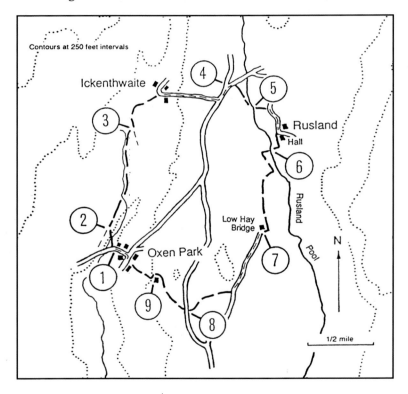

1   A few yards along the road from the village hall, in the direction of Lowick, is a trackway leading off to the right signposted as leading to Stock Farm. Within two hundred yards the track branches in two. Follow the left-hand branch which fords a stream. Within another few hundred yards this joins another trackway. (1/4 mile)

2 Here turn right and follow the trackway northwards to Ickenthwaite. The route soon becomes a confusion of trackways but fortunately the bridleway you should be following, which soon becomes a rough pathway, is well way-marked with a series of arrows. Eventually it joins another trackway. (3/4 mile)

3 Here turn left. The track eventually reaches a narrow roadway at the hamlet of Ickenthwaite. Here turn right. The road descends downhill and eventually reaches a road junction. Here turn left and then take the first turn right on to the Rusland Hall road. (1 mile)

4 Within a hundred yards along this road a trackway leads off to the right. Some two hundred yards along this trackway, just before reaching the river Rusland Pool, is a kissing gate next to a six bar gate on the right-hand side of the track. Pass through the kissing gate and turn left to follow the left-hand side of the field you enter to another kissing gate which gives access to a foot-bridge crossing Rusland Pool. (1/4 mile)

5 On the other side of the river is the terminus of a trackway. Here turn right and follow the trackway to a roadway. Here turn right and follow the road to the gate house of Rusland Hall. Here bear right again on to a trackway lead-ing round the back of Rusland Hall and signposted as being a public footpath leading to Bouth and Oxen Park. This leads to a bridge spanning Rusland Pool. (1/2 mile)

6 On the other side of the bridge is a signposted footpath leading off to the left which follows a series of waymark posts. About a quarter of a mile from the bridge the path appears to branch in two. Bear right following a series of white posts leading through some woodland. The path finally emerges from the wood by way of a foot bridge leading to a house called Low Hay Bridge. (1/2 mile)

7 Follow the narrow surfaced road leading uphill from the house, signposted as being a footpath leading to Bouth. A few hundred yards after crossing a cat-tlegrid a lone signpost indicates a footpath leading uphill to the right. There is little or no evidence of a path but fortunately the right of way is waymarked with a series of waymark posts which lead to a metal gate, through which it then follows the wall to your left, through two more gates, to a roadway. (1 mile)

8 Here turn right. Fifty yards along the road is a signpost indicating a public footpath leading off to the left to a six bar gate. From the gate the right of way heads directly towards the farm you see ahead of you, by way of two more gates. Passing the right-hand side of the farm complex the right of way comes to the farm's driveway. (1/2 mile)

9 Turn left. Walk fifteen yards into the farmyard and turn right through a metal gate and follow the left-hand side of the field you enter to another metal gate. Pass through this gate and follow the wall to your right back to Oxen Park village. (1/4 mile)

POTTER TARN

Distance	4 3/4 miles
Total feet of Ascent	700 feet
Suggested time	2 1/2 hours
Starting point	Staveley Village
	4 miles east of Windermere (SD 470 983)
Car Parking	Centre of village

This walk is a pleasant ramble through pastoral scenery with some very grand views of the fells to the north, at the head of the Kentmere valley and away westwards to Langdale, and concludes with a riverside walk back to Staveley. Potter Tarn itself is something of a curiosity, and is more curious still if you examine closely the course of its outflow.

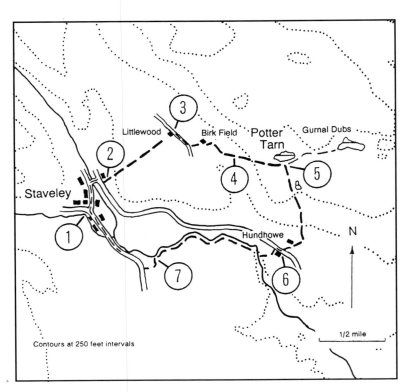

1   From the small car park in the centre of the village, next to the telephone box, follow the road veering northwards off the village main street and signposted as leading to Kentmere. A quarter of a mile along this road another road branches off to the right across a bridge, signposted as leading to Burnside.

After crossing the bridge the road curves to the right. Almost on the curve of this bend, going off to the left, past a cottage called Riverside, is a small driveway which appears to be private but is a right of way leading to a kissing gate. (1/4 mile)

2   From the kissing gate a path leads directly up the fellside crossing a series of solidly constructed tall wooden wall stiles that also serve as very effective waymarks. Dipping downhill on the other side of the fell the path comes to a secluded little farmstead called Littlewood Farm. (3/4 miles)

3   On reaching the road passing by the farm turn right. A few hundred yards along the road a trackway leads off to the left to Birk Field Farm. Reaching the farm a right of way continues past the front of the farm house and then continues along a distinctive rustic trackway initially following a stream and then pulling uphill to a metal gate. (1/2 mile)

4   Beyond the gate is a more distinct trackway. Here turn right. 20 yards along the track a steep path leads uphill to the left through a rock strewn fellside. Although a grassy path it is fairly easy to follow. Where it isn't simply keep walking straight ahead and you should soon arrive at Potter Tarn. (1/2 mile)

(This walk can be lengthened by including a visit to Gurnal Dubs which is surprisingly Scottish in appearance. To do so cross the outflow of the tarn and follow a path leading to a large slate wall stile. From this stile the path continues across the fells to the east of Potter Tarn directly to Gurnal Dubs. The walk there and back puts another mile on the walk.)

5   From the outflow of the tarn follow a grassy trackway leading downhill. As you draw level with a large farm complex to your right, called Hundhowe, begin looking for a gateway on your right from which begins an enclosed pathway that leads to it. From its farmyard a trackway leads down the roadway. (3/4 mile)

6   Here turn right. A hundred yards along the road an indicated right of way sign points left to a trackway leading through Hagg Foot Farm down to a bridge crossing the river Kent. Once across the river continue along a pathway that follows the south bank of the river upstream back towards Staveley. A quarter of a mile before reaching the farm the track leads to, where there is a sharp bend in the river, the right of way has been diverted left from the track to a kissing gate. (1 1/4 miles)

7   Passing through the kissing gate the right of way follows the right-hand edge of the field you have just entered to a second kissing gate through which it continues along a trackway to join the main road through Staveley. Here turn right to return back to the centre of the village. (3/4 mile)

SCHOOL KNOTT

Distance	5 1/2 miles
Total feet of Ascent	500 feet
Suggested time	2 1/2 hours
Starting point	Ings village, 2 miles east of Windermere (SD 445 987)
Car Parking	See first directional note

The terrain covered by this little walk is like the surface of a rumpled cloth, full of dips and little hillocks providing a great variety of scenery. Frequently great sweeping panoramas of distant hills open up as you come to the top of a rise, particularly from School Knott itself which looks over Windermere and Windermere Lake. Interspersed between these views are the more intimate pleasures of attractive dells and wooded glades.

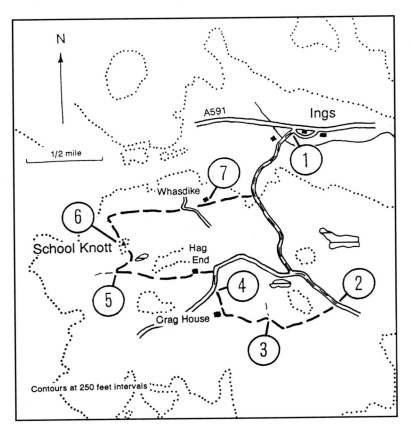

1   Travelling from Windermere turn right off the main A591 just before Ings Church and turn first right on to a road simply indicated as a gated road. The initial part of this road is broad enough to park on. Continue along this road which is surprisingly narrow and pleasantly unenclosed. Eventually it links in to another road. Here turn left. Follow this second road for almost half a mile to the start of an enclosed bridleway leading off to the right signposted as being part of the Dales Way. (1 3/4 miles)

2   The bridleway leads to a metal gate but it is a metal gate ten yards before this, in the righthand wall, through which the bridleway actually continues as a grassy trackway initially following the other side of the wall and then veering away from it slightly. Within a few hundred yards the track comes to curve round a small copse of conifer trees. At the far end of this copse, just before it crosses a small stream flowing out of the copse, another trackway veers off to the left initially following the stream. (1/2 mile)

3   The trackway leads to the large farm you can see ahead of you called Crag House. On reaching the farm's first outbuilding locate another trackway leading away to the right and signposted as being a continuation of the Dales Way. This leads to a roadway. (1/2 mile)

4   Here turn right. A couple of hundred yards along the road is a farm access road leading to Hag End Farm, once more signposted as being part of the Dales Way. Entering the farmyard the Dales Way is signposted as continuing past the corrugated end of one of the farm's outbuildings. This is a grassy path but reasonably discernible. After pulling uphill a little it then leads downhill to a six bar gate and kissing gate. (3/4 mile)

5   After passing through either of these gates turn right. A very grassy path climbs uphill following a small stream which flows from a delightful little tarn. On reaching the tarn veer uphill to the left towards another six bar gate and kissing gate. From there continue straight ahead to the top of School Knott. (1/4 mile)

6   Continue over School Knott and downhill the other side. Where the path comes to a wall stile do not cross the stile but turn right to follow a path leading eastwards. Again this is a very grassy path which needs some attention to follow it correctly. It takes a more or less straight line through a pleasing glade of birch trees where it leads to a very inconspicuous stone wall stile. Thereon the route is waymarked with yellow arrows and links up to a driveway leading to a large farm you can see straight ahead called Whasdike. (1 mile)

7   Where the drive turns into the yard of the farm an indicated bridleway leads off to the right. This follows the side of a wall leading to a six bar gate giving access to a small copse. After passing through the wood continue walking straight ahead to link up with the road you started out on. Here turn left to return back to Ings. (1 mile)

THE WINSTER VALLEY

Distance	7 miles
Total feet of Ascent	500 feet
Suggested time	3 hours
Starting point	Winster Church
	3 miles south of Windermere (SD 417 930)
Car Parking	In front of church

A countryside walk above and through a peaceful sylvan valley, with the major advantage of visiting, half way round, perhaps the most attractive public house in Lakeland and certainly its most distinctive, having a range of bottled beers that perhaps excels any other pub in the country.

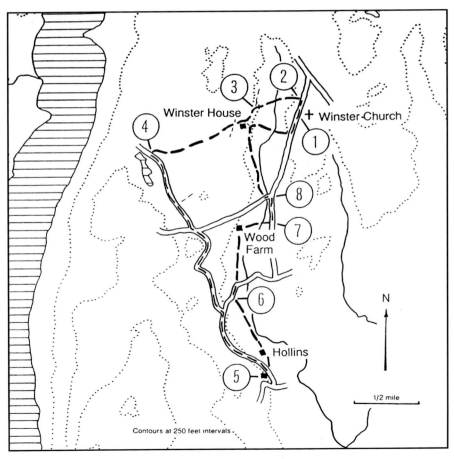

1   From the church walk north in the Windermere direction. Just before reaching a farmstead a signpost points to the start of a footpath leading off to the left beginning from a slate stile. (1/4 mile)

2   The path follows a direct line parallel to a series of walls through a narrow belt of trees to a footbridge. From the bridge it continues along the righthand edge of the field you enter at the top of which is located a slate stile next to a 'hog hole', a hole in the wall which, despite the name, is meant for sheep to pass through. Another slate stile is to be seen directly ahead. A few yards from this second stile the path comes to a grassy trackway. (1/2 mile)

3   Here turn left. On reaching the large stable block of Winster House continue along a trackway that leads uphill to the right. Passing through a six bar gate it comes to a junction with another trackway. At this point veering just slightly to the left continue ahead along an initially imperceptible pathway signposted as leading to Ghyll Head. After a few hundred yards this becomes a distinctive path finally leading to a roadway. (1 mile)

4   Here turn left. Half a mile along the road a gated road leads off to the left. Ignore this turning. On reaching a road junction turn left. Do not turn down the road with the 'Deep Ford' sign, likewise ignore any turnings to the right or the left but continue following the direction signs to Cartmel Fell until you reach 'The Masons Arms', which though lacking in apostrophes is the cause of many exclamations! (2 1/2 miles)

5   From 'The Masons Arms' continue back along the road you arrived on. A few hundred yards from the pub branch right on to a signposted bridleway for Hollins Farm. The right of way passes in front of the farm and then between two outbuildings. From thereon it is easy to follow until you enter a broad field. Here continue straight forward to a five bar gate at the opposite end of the field. From there the bridleway quickly comes to a roadway. (1 mile)

6   Turn right. Within three hundred yards a signpost points to a bridleway leading off to the left to Wood Farm. This is mostly an indistinct path but takes a more or less direct course to the first farm building you can see ahead of you. On reaching Wood Farm follow the farm's access road, right, to a roadway. (3/4 mile)

7   On reaching the road turn left. A quarter of a mile along the road another road branches off to the left through a deep ford. Fortunately next to it there is a slate bridge for walkers to use. Almost immediately after crossing the bridge, to the right, is the start of a signposted pathway. (1/4 mile)

8   To begin with this is actually a trackway but three hundred yards or so from the road, after passing through a currently gateless gateway, the right of way follows a distinct footpath branching off to the right. After crossing a stream it veers uphill to the left slightly and becomes more of a grassy trackway eventually reaching the driveway to Winster House. Turn right. On reaching the road turn left to return to the walk's starting point. (1 1/4 miles)

WHITBARROW SCAR

Distance	4 1/2 miles
Total feet of Ascent	800 feet
Suggested time	2 1/2 hours
Starting point	Witherslack Hall, 6 miles SW of Kendal (SD 437 859)
Car Parking	100 yards along the track the walk begins on

Whitbarrow is a large, attractive and intriguing limestone hill bounded by a huge cliff and quite unlike the rest of the Lake District. A good part of it is a nature reserve and for the natural historian the place is a treasure trove of interest. From its top, on a good day, are to be seen sweeping views of the Lakeland fells, the Howgills, Morecambe Bay and the Pennines.

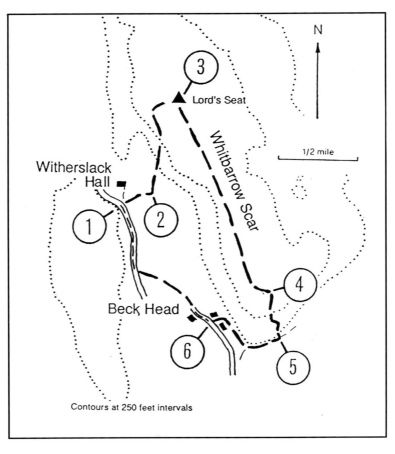

1   From the entrance of Witherslack Hall School follow the broad trackway that leads off to the right signposted as leading to Whitbarrow. Passing through a gateway the path branches in two. Bear left. Where it splits in two again this time bear right towards a football field. At the far end of the playing pitch a stile gives access to a waymarked path that leads across the playing pitch behind the goal posts. (1/4 mile)

2   From the playing field the path leads into the wood behind it and then pulls steeply uphill. Where it begins to level the path makes a sharp right hand turn and following a line of cairns leads directly to the summit of Whitbarrow, Lord's Seat, which is marked with a robust memorial cairn to Canon G. A. K. Hervey. (3/4 mile)

    (The wood directly to the east of Lord's Seat is an fascinating place to explore but you are almost guaranteed to get lost if you do so! To enter it follow the path that leads north from the cairn. If however you are not prepared to become disorientated then ignore this passage and go on to directional note 3 below.)

3   From the summit cairn head south in the direction of Morecambe Bay along a distinct pathway which after crossing a wooden stile follows the edge of a thick plantation of conifers. Shortly after curving eastwards round the edge of this plantation, after gaining a full view of the river Kent and its wide meanders, the path swings sharply downhill to the right. (1 1/2 miles)

4   On its descent the path passes through a limestone wall, turns left and passes back through the wall again and then runs diagonally downhill. Where it may seem to branch in two always choose the lower option. Eventually at the foot of its descent the path reaches a broad trackway. (1/4 mile)

5   Here turn right. A few hundred yards along the trackway, just before it curves left, leading off to the right is another trackway signposted as being a public footpath to the hamlet of Beck Head. Reaching the hamlet the path concludes by passing along the side of a conservatory belonging to a long white house and then follows the driveway of the house down to a narrow road. (1/2 mile)

6   Here turn right. Passing the last house in the hamlet the road becomes an unsurfaced trackway. Where it joins a surfaced road turn right. Witherslack Hall is half a mile along the road. (1 mile)

SCOUT SCAR

Distance	5 1/4 miles
Total feet of Ascent	800 feet
Suggested time	3 hours
Starting point	Underbarrow Village
	3 miles west of Kendal (SD 468 922)

This area just west of Kendal is more like the Yorkshire Dales than to the rest of the Lake District as much of it is limestone. Scout Scar in fact is quite an impressive little limestone escarpment from which there are good views of the Lakeland fells. The walk has a number of surprising and pleasant sections, and most importantly like all good walks it begins and ends at a village pub.

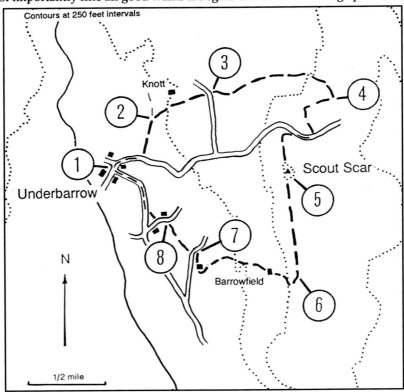

1   Beginning from the village inn in Underbarrow walk eastwards along the road towards Kendal. Three hundred yards along the road leading off to the left is a surfaced driveway to Tranthwaite Hall signposted as being a public footpath. A quarter of a mile along the driveway, on the right, beginning from a kissing gate, is the start of a signposted footpath. (1/2 mile)

2 Although this right of way has quite a number of waymarks it is still fairly difficult to follow as there is little sign of it on the ground. To begin with it veers leftwards and seems as if it may follow a trackway leading into Knott Farm, but instead follows the outer wall of the field enclosing the farm uphill to a kissing gate which gives access to the corner of another field. Continue across this field at an angle that bisects the field's corner. This way you should locate some waymarks which should lead you to a surfaced driveway at a point where a signpost points back to the path you have just followed. (1/2 mile)

3 Immediately on the other side of the road another signpost points to an enclosed trackway, Gamblesmire Lane, which leads up to Cunswick Scar on which an aerial mast is positioned. On reaching the top of this escarpment the track comes to a currently gateless gap in a long limestone wall where there is another signpost. (1 mile)

4 Pass through the gap and turn right to continue along the indicated permissive path which follows the side of the wall you have just passed through towards the aerial mast. Passing through a kissing gate turn left to link onto the driveway leading to the mast which in turn links on to the Underbarrow to Kendal road. Here turn right. A few hundred yards along the road, just as it begins to dip downhill, leading off to the left, through a metal kissing gate, is a very distinct path leading to the top of Scout Scar which is topped by a very ornate shelter. (1 mile)

5 Continue along the path following the edge of the Scout Scar escarpment. As soon as you draw level with Barrowfield Farm, a large farm complex at the foot of the escarpment, begin looking for a large piles of stones that sits almost in the middle of the path and marks the point where the path is crossed by another path moving east to west. (3/4 mile)

6 Follow this new path over the edge of the escarpment down to Barrowfield Farm. From the gable end of the farm house is the start of a signposted path leading directly downhill to Garth Row Lane. This path is well waymarked and leads to a secluded house called Hollin Garth where it moves round the garden of the house and then continues along the house's driveway to reach a roadway. (1 mile)

7 Turn left. Within a matter of yards a footpath is signposted as going off to the right. Head for the far corner of the field you enter to a gateway. Continue the same line across the second field to a stone wall stile. Then, after crossing a stream flowing through this third field, veer right to a roadway. (1/4 mile)

8 Here turn left. Within two hundred yards a signpost, pointing right, indicates a right of way along a driveway leading to a house called Rockyfield where it continues as a grassy path along the side of a wall to a roadway. Here turn right. On reaching a road junction turn right again. The Punchbowl Inn is a hundred yards on. (1/2 mile)

HAMPSFIELD FELL

Distance	5 1/2 miles
Total feet of Ascent	700 feet
Suggested time	3 hours
Starting point	Cartmel Village, 12 miles south of Windermere (SD 378 788)
Car Parking	100 yards from the village centre

Hampsfield Fell is the southernmost fell in the Lake District National Park and has marvellous views of Morecambe Bay to the south and the Lakeland Fells to the north. The walk's other main virtue is that it begins from Cartmel, the most attractive village in Cumbria possessing the county's most magnificent building, Cartmel Priory.

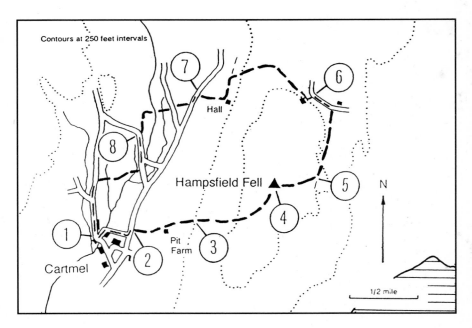

1   From the centre of the village follow the road leading under the gatehouse archway. Where it comes to a road junction turn left. Less than forty yards along the road leading off to the right is a signposted public footpath to the 'Hospice of Hampsfell'. (1/4 mile)

2   After passing through a gateway continue directly ahead to Pit Farm the roof of which can just be seen. Reaching the farm the path continues through a

metal gate a few yards to the left of a large metal barn, whence it then veers slightly to the left towards the far corner of the field the gate gives access to. (1/2 mile)

3   Near the corner of the field a signpost indicates that the path continues into the next field through a metal gate and then along the lefthand side of this next field pulling steeply uphill to a metal kissing gate. From here on the path is more distinctive continuing the same direct course uphill. Where it levels, reaching the brow of the ridge, it comes to a crossways with another path. Here turn left. This new path leads directly to the summit of Hampsfield Fell. (3/4 mile)

4   From the doorway of the hospice follow the path leading south-eastwards directly to Grange. Within a few hundred yards observe a long limestone wall to your left. A few hundred yards downhill along the wall is a waymarked stile. Passing over this stile a distinct path leads down hill eventually reaching a trackway. (1/2 mile)

5   Here turn left. The trackway, which is very grassy in parts, follows the edge of Eggerslack Wood and eventually reaches a surfaced roadway. Here turn left. About three hundred yards along the road, where the road curves right, bear left onto a trackway leading into a farmyard. (3/4 mile)

6   Within a few yards the trackway turns sharp right between two rows of farm outbuildings. Where it splits in two bear left. Within a hundred yards or so you are faced with two gates. Just to the left of the righthand gate is a stile. Continuing directly downhill from this stile a second stile is reached. From this second stile the right of way curves round a small copse to your left and becomes a very grassy trackway leading diagonally downhill to join a rough surfaced trackway. Here turn left. The track leads through Hampsfield Hall Farm to a roadway. (1 mile)

7   Here turn left. A hundred yards along the road to the right, just past the main gates of Broughton Lodge, is a stile, the start of a signposted footpath. Follow the righthand edge of the field you enter leading to another stile which gives access to another road. Immediately across the road is a third stile. Once over this again follow the righthand edge of the field you enter to a small slate footbridge and stile. Once again you follow the right hand edge of the next field you enter to another footbridge and stile. Directly ahead is a sixth stile giving access to a small copse. Continue straight ahead through the copse until you reach a pond. Here the path turns sharp left exits the copse and heads almost directly for the tower of the priory finally reaching a roadway. (1/2 mile)

8   Here turn left. A quarter of a mile along the road, opposite an old mill, is the start of a signposted bridleway leading off to the right through a wicket gate. Crossing another slate bridge the path follows the left hand edge of the field you enter to a six bar gate. After passing through the gate follow the righthand edge of the next two fields which leads you to a stream. A few yards upstream is another slate bridge. Continue straight ahead from the bridge to a gateway at the top of the field which gives access to a road. Here turn left and follow the road back to Cartmel. (1 mile)

BLETHECAR MOOR

Distance	4 1/2 miles
Total feet of Ascent	700 feet
Suggested time	2 1/2 hours
Starting Point	Nibthwaite Village
	6 miles south of Coniston (SD 294 897)

After a steep ascent this walk crosses Blethecar Moor, a wild mountain moorland fell, in order to reach a remarkable trackway leading to High and Low Parkamoor, two of the most improbably positioned farmsteads in the Lake District. This trackway serves as a wonderful elevated walkway with superb views overlooking Coniston Water and the Coniston Fells beyond.

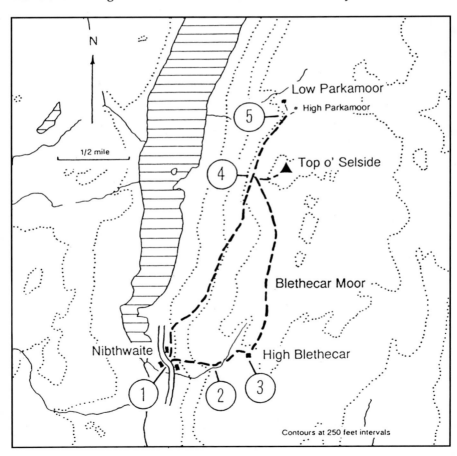

1   Beginning from the village phone box, facing north, follow the right of way leading off to the right up a narrow tarmacked driveway which a wooden signpost next to the post box points to. Within a few yards the drive comes to a five bar gate. Passing through the gate turn immediately right to follow a path initially following the wall you have just passed through. This is an easy, though steep path to follow, until it comes to a stream which the path appears to cross in order to pass through a metal gate on the other side. (1/2 mile)

2   The right of way does not cross the stream at this point however but continues upstream another hundred yards or so and then crosses it. It continues along the stream another short distance and then veers away to the right along a stone wall which leads to a tall wall stile next to a metal gate. Cross over the stile and follow the grassy trackway on the other side to High Blethecar Farm. (1/4 mile)

3   Leading uphill from the farm, initially following a small stream, is a pathway leading to a small gateway. From the gateway onwards the path is much clearer and within a few hundred yards links on to another path leading northwards, which crosses the mountain moorland terrain of Blethecar Fell eventually reaching a rough trackway. (1 1/4 miles)

     (About 50 yards before joining this trackway an almost imperceptible path veers off to the right and leads to the Top o' Selside, the highest point between Coniston Water and Windermere. This diversion adds another 300 feet of ascent and half a mile's extra walking to the walk. Though the view is not very spectacular from the top it requires so little effort to reach it is probably worth doing.)

4   On reaching the Parkamoor track follow it northwards at least as far as the point where it branches in two where you can see Low Parkamoor Farm and large stretches of Coniston Water. (1/2 mile)

5   Having viewed Low Parkamoor (or perhaps chosen to go on to view it at close hand) turn round and follow the trackway southwards back to Nibthwaite. (2 miles)

TARN HOWS

Distance	5 1/2 miles
Total feet of Ascent	800 feet
Suggested time	3 hours
Starting point	Tarn Hows Car Park
	2 miles NE of Coniston (SD 326 995)

Tarn Hows is one of Lakeland's premier 'beauty spots', it has a very rugged set-ting which this walk explores. For once the conifer trees which are present in this landscape actually seem to enhance its appeal, at least in parts, to give it a slightly Alpine look. Despite the fact that it has to parallel a main road at one stage this walk has a very adventurous feel to it with a number of surprises and lots of good views generally.

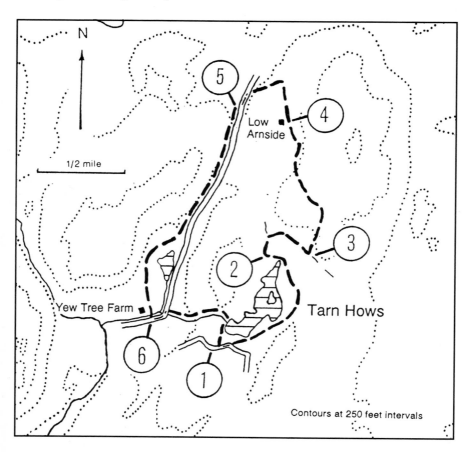

1   Starting from the main entrance of the National Trust Tarn Hows car park turn right. Just before reaching the second 'Passing Place' sign, about two hundred yards from the car park entrance, veering off to the left is the start of a trackway. Keep to this broad path signed at one point as the main path around the tarn. Coming round the far end of the tarn the path splits in three. (1 mile)

2   A small sign indicates that it is the middle path which is the main path around the lake, but at this point follow the path leading away to the right. This leads to a broad enclosed trackway. Here turn right. Just over a quarter of a mile along this trackway another trackway leads off to the left signposted as being a bridleway. (1/2 mile)

3   After a short passage through some dense afforestation the path crosses some rough open enclosures to eventually join a trackway leading from an isolated farm called Low Arnside. (1 mile)

4   Within a couple of hundred yards from the farm the track leading from the farm branches in two. Bear left. The track soon becomes a very grassy path. Leading through a gateway however it becomes somewhat more obvious leading directly downhill and is waymarked with a number of currently weathered yellow waymarks. After a descent of two to three hundred feet the path becomes a broad trackway which veers to the left and within three hundred yards joins the main Ambleside to Coniston road. (1/2 mile)

5   Here turn left. Within one hundred yards, on the righthand side of the road, is a tall wooden stile crossing a stone wall. After crossing this stile turn left. The path parallels the main road, crossing on the way the driveway to High Oxen Fell. About one mile from the start, waymarked with a series of white arrows, the path begins to veer right away from the road and gains some height. Passing through a six bar gate however it veers left, downhill, to rejoin the road again at Yew Tree Farm. (1 3/4 miles)

6   Turn left. Two hundred yards along the road immediately after crossing a bridge is the start of a footpath signposted as leading to Tarn Hows following upstream the side of the beck the bridge crosses. (Within twenty yards either side of the bridge is the start of three paths, so be sure to follow the middle sign post which is the correct one.) Where the path splits in two keep to the branch which keeps closest to the stream. On reaching Tarn Hows turn right. After passing through a gateway keep to the broader path ahead of you. On reaching the roadway the car park is directly ahead of you. (3/4 mile)

BLAWITH KNOTT

Distance	6 miles
Total feet of Ascent	800 feet
Suggested time	3 hours
Starting point	Blawith Church, 6 miles south of Coniston (SD 289 883)
Car Parking	In front of church

A walk using unenclosed roads and bridleways circuiting a rugged rambling fell with wide spacious vistas of other distant fells and the open sea. Amidst this unpromising fell land are a surprising number of near isolated farmsteads whose green fields stand in sharp contrast to the open fell and cause one to wonder at the past hard labours that must have gone into their creation.

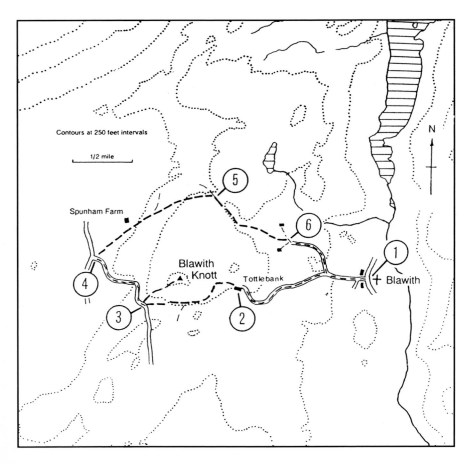

1   Opposite the phone box, next to the church, is the start of a road leading westwards from the main road. Within a hundred yards the road branches in two. Continue along the righthand branch. After another half mile the road branches in two again. This time bear left. Reaching Tottlebank, a former farmstead, the road becomes unsurfaced and continues as a rough trackway signposted as being a bridleway. (1 1/4 miles)

2   Half a mile from Tottlebank the track curves left, but continuing straight forward, in the direction of Black Combe, is a grassier trackway. Continue along this trackway which eventually joins a roadway. (1 mile)

3   Here turn right. *(Within fifty yards along the road is the start of a trackway leading off to the right which soon reduces to a pathway leading to the top of Blawith Knott. This diversion to the top and back adds another 3/4 of a mile to the walk and an extra 400 feet of climbing. Once back on the road, or having chosen not to take this option...)* Follow the road downhill. Almost at the foot of the road's descent, just before it comes to a road junction, a partly tarmacked trackway leads off to the right, signposted as being a public bridleway. (3/4 mile)

4   Continue along this partially tarmacked trackway. A hundred yards or so before it reaches Spunham Farm a small sign with the word 'bridleway' indicates a grassier trackway veering off to the right. Within four hundred yards it branches in two. Bear right. After pulling uphill and then dropping downhill slightly this path links up with another bridleway. (1 1/4 miles)

5   Here turn right. Within a few hundred yards the path branches in two. Bear right. After a very soggy section the path becomes a distinct trackway eventually reaching a surfaced driveway. (3/4 mile)

6   Follow the driveway downhill. In the space of a few yards a driveway leading from Appletree Holme Farm links in to it and the driveway becomes a narrow surfaced roadway. On reaching the road junction you were at earlier turn left and return to Blawith Church. (1 mile)

WATER YEAT TO CONISTON.

Distance	7 miles
Total feet of Ascent	750 feet
Suggested time	3 hours
Starting point	Water Yeat, 5 miles south of Coniston (SD 289 891)

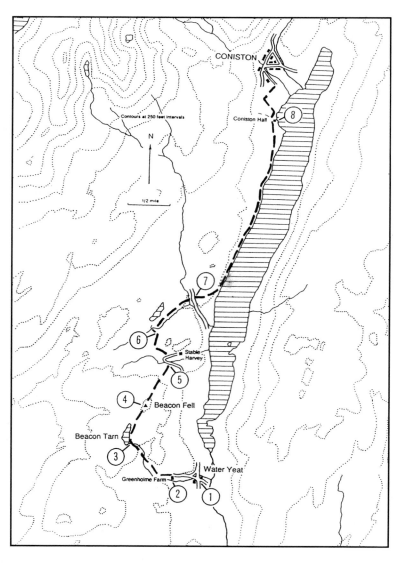

As this is a linear walk, and requires the use of public or private transport, see page 5, to reach the starting point at Water Yeat. This is a walk in two distinct sections. Firstly across the Blawith Fells which have a surprisingly mountainous feet to them and then a more gentle section along the western shore of Coniston Water

1   Beginning from the roadsign in the middle of the hamlet follow the unsign-posted road leading westwards to the village hall, where the road branches in two, and bear left. The road is surfaced as far as Greenholme Farm. (1/2 mile)

2   From Greenholme Farm onwards the route continues as a rough trackway. Within a few yards the trackway branches in two. Bear left. The trackway reduces to a footpath as it crosses Blawith Common. A number of paths branch off to the left and the right but stick to the path which looks the most distinctive. This will eventually bring you to Beacon Tarn. (3/4 mile)

3   Continue along a path that initially follows the eastern side of the tarn and then veers away to the right heading for the top of Beacon Fell. (1/2 mile))

4   From the top of the summit a distinct path leads downhill on the other side which unfortunately soon begins bifurcating and producing a number of confusing alternatives. Choose the option which seems to be heading most directly towards Stable Harvey, the isolated farmstead positioned almost on top of the green hillock ahead of you. This should eventually bring you to the curving access road leading to the farm. (1/2 mile)

5   On reaching the access road turn left. Just after the road turns sharp right are to be found two sign posts. Follow the second one indicating a bridleway leading off to the left . There soon develops a confusing number of trackways. Follow the one which appears to be the most direct and follows a line of electricity poles. Just after the track turns sharply left it passes under another line of electricity cables. (1/2 mile.)

6   Almost exactly at this point a grassy path veers off to the right crosses a stream and then continues down the valley the stream flows down, on its northern side, eventually reaching the A5084. (1/2 mile)

7   Immediately on the other side of the road is a signpost indicating a right of way along a trackway leading towards Coniston Water. On reaching the lakeshore the right of way becomes a footpath and follows the lakeshore northwards eventually merging into a driveway leading to Coniston Hall. (2 1/2 miles)

8   Beyond Coniston Hall, and passing between two outbuildings, a trackway veers off to the right from the driveway. The track takes a zigzagged route to Coniston Village, reducing in its final few hundred yards to a footpath as it reaches the road passing Coniston's secondary school. (3/4 miles)

CLAIFE HEIGHTS

Distance	8 miles
Total feet of Ascent	1000 feet
Suggested time	4 hours
Starting point	Far Sawrey, 3 miles S W of Windermere (SD 379 954)
Car Parking	In front of village hall

This is a very varied walk including perhaps the most attractive part of the Windermere shoreline, followed by a section of country lane walking and concluding with a easy ramble across the intriguing open landscape of Claife Heights.

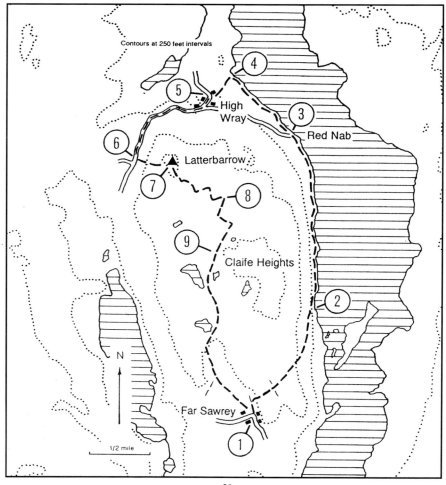

1   Directly opposite the entrance to the village hall, the former village school, next to a phone box, is the start of a trackway leading off to the left. Where the track splits in two, within three hundred yards from the start, bear right. After another quarter of a mile the track comes to a crossways with another path. Continue straight ahead. The track is now signposted as leading to the lake shore. (1 mile)

2   On reaching the Windermere shoreline turn left and continue along a broad trackway that follows the shoreline northwards. Eventually, passing through a gateway at Red Nab the track becomes surfaced. At this point veering off to the right is a short trackway leading to a small car park. (1 3/4 miles)

3   Beginning from the northern end of the car park is a trackway which continues along the lake shore signposted as leading to Wray Church. From the second boathouse you come to along the shoreline leading uphill to the left is the start of a path signposted as leading to High Wray. (3/4 mile)

4   Confusingly this path parallels a more distinct, but private, path on the other side of the wall the public right of way follows. Keep to the right hand boundary of the two fields the right of way crosses. Finally, following the side of a tall garden wall, the path comes to a slate stile. It may seem as if this stile gives access to private land, but the other side is a public right of way. Immediately after crossing the stile turn right to join a roadway. (1/4 mile)

5   Here turn left. One and a quarter miles along this road, at the top of a slight rise, one hundred yards before a road junction, leading off to the left, through a six bar gate, is the start of a signposted footpath. (1 mile)

6   The path pulls steeply uphill. Some two hundred yards from the start a thinner path leads off to the left leading to the top of Latterbarrow. (1/4 mile)

7   From the summit cairn continue along a path that leads southwards, in the opposite direction to Ambleside, downhill to a stile crossing a wire fence which gives access to a distinct path leading away to the left. This path takes a very convoluted course through thick afforestation but is very well way-marked with a series of white topped posts. Eventually it reaches a signpost. Here the path joins a bridleway. Turn left, as the signpost indicates this is the direction to follow in order to return to Far Sawrey. Within four hundred yards the path comes to a forestry road. (1 mile)

8   Here turn right. A quarter of a mile along the road a signpost indicates a bridleway cuts across the road. Here turn right to follow this bridleway back to Sawrey. Within a few hundred yards a forestry track links into the bridleway. Another few hundred yards further on the trackway splits in two. Bear left. Another final few hundred yards and the trackway reaches a five bar gate and one has finally reached the edge of the forest. (1/2 mile)

9   The bridleway continues southwards as a distinct trackway eventually becoming enclosed between two stone walls. Where it splits in two the inevitable signpost indicates you should bear left to return to Far Sawrey. (1 3/4 miles)

STICKLE PIKE

Distance 5 1/2 miles
Total feet of Ascent 1500 feet
Suggested time 3 1/2 hours
Starting point Blacksmith's Arms, Broughton Mills (SD 222 906)
6 1/2 miles SW of Coniston
Car Parking Pub car park with landlord's permission.

Despite its relatively low height Stickle Pike is a true fell walk and requires some skills at navigation. From the top of Stickle Pike there are some dramatic views northwards along the Duddon valley towards the highest peaks in Cumbria and southwards towards the Duddon Estuary.

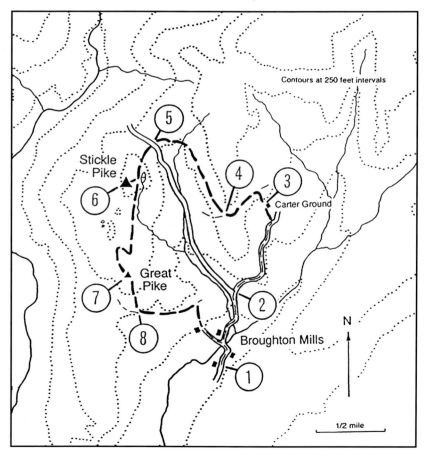

1   From the pub turn left and follow the road downhill. Once over the bridge bear right and follow the signpost to Seathwaite. After pulling uphill a short distance take the first turn right. (1/2 mile)

2   Three quarters of a mile along this road a signpost indicates a public bridleway leading off to the left along a driveway to Carter Ground Farm. Crossing a cattlegrid the right of way continues past the front of the lefthand domicile and through the garden of the house to a metal gate. (1 mile)

3   From the gate onwards the bridleway is not very discernible and overgrown with reeds. It veers slightly left to begin with and then takes a weaving course directly uphill becoming slightly more discernible and rutted in places. About two hundred yards from the metal gate it joins another very indistinct bridleway. The junction is marked with a small cairn. Here turn left. The path soon becomes clearer. Reaching the remains of a moribund wall almost imperceptibly the path branches in two. (1/2 mile)

4   Bear right. After curving round the head of a field of rough pasture the path crosses a broad trackway, pulls uphill slightly and passes through some old mine workings and eventually reaches the Seathwaite road. (1 mile)

5   On the other side of the road a path continues directly ahead. About a hundred yards from the road it branches in two. Bear left on to the branch leading uphill. A hundred yards or so after passing Stickle Tarn a worn path veers off to the right to the top of Stickle Pike. (1/2 mile)

6   Return back to the path which the summit path veers off from and turn right. This path is quite distinct until it reaches the base of a steep bank where it branches in two. Each branch veers off at a right angle. Bear right. The path soon comes to a crossways with another path. Bear left on to the new path. About a hundred yards or so after passing a small group of tarns veer left off the path, more or less making your own course as there is no distinct path to follow, towards the trig point on the top of Great Stickle. (1 mile)

7   Continue downhill from Great Stickle in the direction of the Duddon Estuary. Again there is no distinct path to begin with though you should be able to locate one as you descend. The end of the descent brings you to a trackway running along the side of a stone wall. (1/4 mile)

8   Here turn left. The track soon passes through a gateway. About seven hundred yards further on it reaches a picnic table(!). Here the track branches in two. Bear right onto the branch which leads downhill. Within a few hundred yards the track becomes surfaced and eventually joins the road which you started out on. Here turn right to return back to the start of the walk. (1 mile)

THE YEWDALE FELLS

Distance	6 1/2 miles
Total feet of Ascent	1500 feet
Suggested time	4 hours
Starting point	Coniston Car Park (SD 303 976)

The Coniston fells present perhaps the boldest bulwark of rock and crag in the Lake District. This walk explores a little of that rugged landscape. It is not then a walk for the novice walker, even though the start of the walk is surprisingly pastoral.

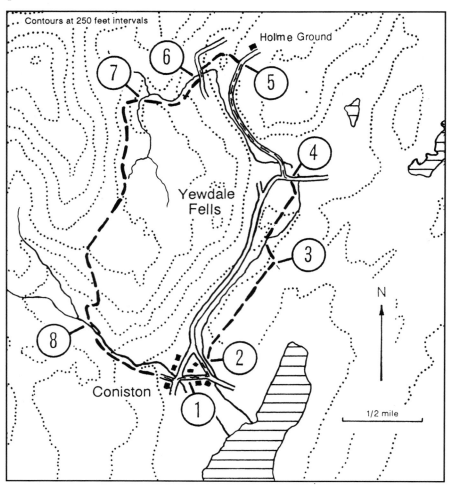

1   On leaving the car park turn left and then turn right on to the Hawkshead road. Two hundred yards along the road turn left on to a road signposted as leading to Ambleside. Follow the road as far as the junior school where a signposted footpath leads off to the right across a small stone bridge spanning Yewdale Beck. (1/4 mile)

2   Once across the bridge the right of way follows the beck a few yards upstream and then veers off to the right. This is a distinct path which crosses over a small wooded hillock. On the descent side of the hillock the path is waymarked with a series of yellow arrows. Eventually the path reaches a rough trackway. (3/4 mile)

3   Here turn left. After crossing a stone bridge bear right on to a trackway which passes the fronts of three cottages and leads to a six bar gate. From here on the right of way continues forward as a pathway in a fairly direct line through a series of gates until it reaches the end of another trackway. Here turn left and follow the trackway to the main Coniston to Ambleside road. (3/4 mile)

4   Here turn left. A hundred yards along the road turn right on to a road signposted as leading to Hodge Close. A mile along this road, just after Holme Ground Farm comes into view, a trackway leads off to the left signposted as being a public footpath. Do not confuse this trackway with another trackway which veers off to the left a hundred yards before but which is unsignposted. (1 mile)

5   A hundred yards or so along this trackway, just before reaching a six bar gate, a narrow path leads off to the left signposted as leading to Tilberthwaite car park. On reaching the roadway next to which the car park is positioned turn left. A hundred yards along the road, leading off to the right, is a flight of steps leading to a broad pathway. (1/4 mile)

6   This is a straightforward path to follow until it branches in three different directions, the left branch obviously leading into an old quarry and the right branch into Tilberthwaite Gill. Choose the middle branch which continues uphill and leads round the head of the gorge where it fords Crook Beck, one of the two main becks which flow into it. (1/2 mile)

7   Ten yards from the beck the path becomes very grassy as it branches in two. Take the left branch, which the author has sought to waymark with a few small cairns. Within a hundred yards this becomes a very distinctive path which, after taking a long course across some very rugged fell land, finally makes a steep descent so as to link up with the old access road leading to the area's former copper mines. (2 miles)

8   Here turn left. Two to three hundred yards downhill bear right over the Miners' Bridge spanning Church Beck on to the track which follows the beck downstream along its western bank. Eventually the track reaches the terminus of a surfaced road which leads back to Coniston. (3/4 mile)

THE CONISTON FELLS

Highest Point	The Old Man of Coniston 2,631 feet
Distance	7 1/2 miles
Total feet of Ascent	3,500 feet
Suggested time	6 hours
Starting point	Coniston, (SD 302 976)
Car Parking	Car park in the middle of the village

This walk is a circuit of fells which provide such a dramatic setting to the village of Coniston. It is a classic fell walk and much harder than any of the other walks described in this guide.

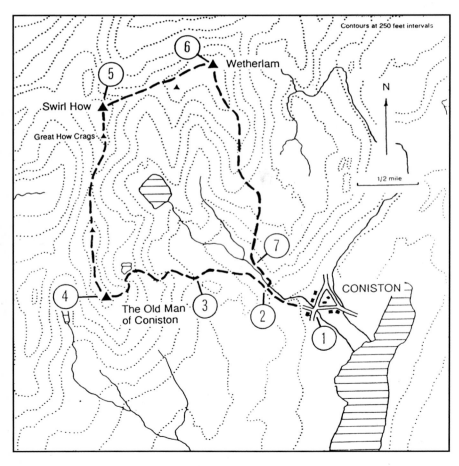

1   Starting from the bridge in the centre of the village, next to Barclays Bank, follow the road signposted as leading to the Sun Hotel. Turn right at the gable end of the hotel up a short access road signposted as leading to the Old Man and Levers Water. At the top end of the access road pass through a small gate next to a directional sign to the Y.H.A. on to a trackway. The track soon comes to a bridge which takes the track over Church Beck. (1/2 mile)

2   Do not cross the bridge but keep to the left hand, western, side of Church Beck following an obvious pathway. Within a few hundred yards of crossing over a stile, the path veers away from Church Beck towards the Old Man of Coniston. After climbing nearly 500 feet the path joins a trackway coming from the left. (3/4 mile)

3   Within 40 yards of joining this trackway another path leads off to the right. Be sure to ignore this turning and keep to the trackway which makes a steep twisting ascent through a complex series of abandoned quarry workings to the summit of the Old Man of Coniston. (1 mile)

4   From the summit head north along a graceful ridge to Swirl How. (1 3/4 miles)

    (In mist is easy to mistake Great How Crags for Swirl How and thereby also mistake a path that leads eastwards from it for the one described below. This is not a proper route and can lead to serious difficulties. If you are therefore unsure as to whether you are on the summit of Swirl How or Great How Crags you would be best advised return back to the Old Man of Coniston.)

5   From the summit of Swirl How descend eastwards to the gap between Swirl How and Wetherlam, and from thence ascend to the summit of Wetherlam itself. (1 mile)

6   From Wetherlam head south along a pleasant ridge descending towards Coniston. Near to the 1,250 foot contour the path joins an old constructed mine path that leads down to an unsurfaced roadway running by the side of Church Beck. (1 3/4 miles)

7   Follow the unsurfaced road towards Coniston. Within a few hundred yards on your right is the bridge which was bypassed at the start of the walk. Cross over the bridge now and return the way you previously came back to Coniston village. (3/4 mile)

(As you return to Coniston village a very pleasant way to conclude the walk is to visit Dixon Ground Farm for a pot of tea. The farm is on your left just before reaching the Sun Hotel. It has an attractive little garden and a very pleasant outlook over Coniston Water.)

CLOSING REMARKS

These final words are included as a result of my meeting with 'Farmer Reg' of Blawith. When I met him he was wearing a battered old hat and was carrying a shovel and bucket and no one could have looked more rustic than he did. I stopped to ask him how docile, or not, was the bull I'd just passed. He made some remark as to how he would just drop the bull's feed over the wall and not tempt his pacidity too much. He then pointed out all the calves the bull had sired in the nearby pen, and how he thought it was more economical to have a bull rather than to depend on the 'AI' man, as the 'AI' man wasn't always successful and he had to be paid whether or not he was.

So we went on talking about one thing and the next. 'Farmer Reg' was a naturally affable person and as he had lived in Blawith all his life there was a lot he could explain about the area. Then he asked what I was doing and I explained. And a slight look of apprehensiveness came over 'Farmer Reg's' countenance.

It seems someone had written a guidebook that had given 'Farmer Reg' no end of problems. It had directed people to walk through one of his gates which they very often forgot to close behind them. There now wasn't a Sunday in the summer that 'Farmer Reg' didn't have to close this particular gate as as a final day's chore. The main transgressors were the Happy Valley Rambling Club and groups of that type, who walk in such long processions that the last one in them always thinks the gates they walk through have been left open by the local farmers rather than the leader of their group. If a gate is meant to be left open it will have a rock propped against it or will be tied back in someway, otherwise you can be almost certain that it should be closed!

Ironically the walk I had just completed surveying before I met 'Farmer Reg' was the only walk I think I've ever surveyed that didn't require the crossing of a single stile or the opening of a single gate. Nevertheless, I promised 'Farmer Reg' that this guidebook would include a special request to all its readers, which I make now:

**Just as you close the cover of this guide onto this page,
please ensure you close all gates behind you.**